DK Simple Science
Science
Experiments
for the very young

DK Simple Science Experiments

for the very young

David Evans

A DORLING KINDERSLEY BOOK

Dorling Kindersley
London • New York • Sydney • Delhi

Editors Veronica Pennycook
Lara Tankel Holtz
Rachel Harrison
U.S. Editor Chuck Wills

Art Editor Jane Horne

Senior Managing Editor Sarah Phillips
Deputy Art Director Mark Richards
DTP Designer Megan Clayton
Production Erica Rosen
Jacket Designer Andrew Nash
Photography Paul Bricknell,
Daniel Pangbourne, and Susanna Price
Consultant and Co-author
Claudette Williams

Published in the United States by
Dorling Kindersley Publishing, Inc.,
95 Madison Avenue, New York, NY 10016

First American Edition, 2000
2 4 6 8 10 7 5 3 1

Copyright © 2000 Dorling Kindersley Limited

0-7894-6165-X

Color reproduction by Colourscan, Singapore
Printed and bound by Graficas Estella, Spain

For our complete catalog visit
WWW.DK.COM

Contents

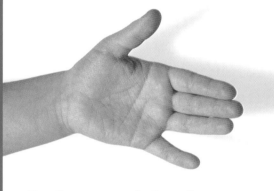

Note to Parents

Young children are always asking questions about the things they see, touch, hear, smell, and taste. **Simple Science Experiments** aims to foster children's natural curiosity and encourages them to use their senses to find out about science. Each chapter features a variety of experiments based on one topic and drawing on a child's everyday experiences. By using familiar and new activities to perform the simple experiments, young children will learn that science plays an important part in the world around them.

About this book

Young children begin to understand science if they are stimulated to think and find out for themselves. This book is designed for you, the parent, to encourage and help your child make his or her own scientific discoveries. A questioning approach is used throughout the book and, wherever possible, results of experiments are not shown. This investigative approach to learning makes science an exciting experience that is not just about acquiring facts.

Equipment

All the experiments can be carried out easily at home with inexpensive materials. Many toy stores stock magnets and the necessary electrical components should be readily available from general electrical or hardware stores. It does not matter if the components are not identical to those shown in this book.

Ways to use this book

At the beginning of each chapter there is an introductory page giving background scientific information and listing key ideas. After the introductory page come the experiments. Every experiment page has an opening paragraph with suggestions for discussions. Before starting an experiment, allow children to help in collecting equipment and to suggest materials to use. Talk about the topic and encourage your child to make predictions about the outcome by asking questions, such as "What do you think will happen?" It is important to let children decide how to carry out the experiment.

Symbols

The following symbols have been used throughout this book:

The Scientific Principles box offers background scientific information that may be useful.

The warning symbol indicates where extra care is needed.

Water and Floating

These experiments enable young children to investigate the nature of water and other liquids. They are encouraged to use all their senses to observe the properties of water and invited to compare water to other liquids.

Children can find out that:

WATER CAN EXIST in different states, i.e., solid (ice), liquid (water), or gas (water vapor), and can change from one state to another.

SOME LIQUIDS MIX with water and some solids dissolve in water.

LIQUIDS CAN FLOW, fill the shape of a container, form drops, and make surfaces wet.

WHEN AN OBJECT MOVES on or through water, the resistance of the water slows down the object.

LIQUIDS EXERT UPWARD FORCES (upthrust), which will cause an object to float unless gravity exerts a greater downward force.

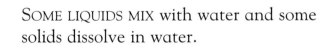

What is water like?

Explore what water tastes, feels, smells, and sounds like. Ask your child about his experience of water—for example, swimming in the sea or walking in the rain. Ask him to describe the smell, sound, feel, or taste.

What does water smell like?

carbonated mineral water

tap water

still mineral water

salty water

Compare the tastes of different types of water. Does mineral water taste the same as tap water? What does water taste like when you add salt to it?

What sound does water make when you pour it?

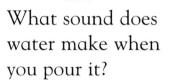

What does water look like?

Scientific Principles

Water is a liquid. It does not have a strong taste or smell and it is colorless.

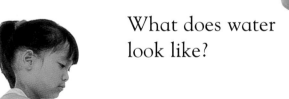

What does water feel like if you wear woolen gloves, or rubber gloves?

It is dangerous to leave children unattended in a wading pool.

Will it mix with water?

Find out more about liquids and investigate what things will mix with water. Ask your child what different liquids she can find in the kitchen, such as vegetable oil, vinegar, or fruit juice. Talk about how to make drinks such as juice, tea, or coffee.

Gather together some different liquids. Do all liquids smell the same? Do all liquids pour?

vinegar

syrup

vegetable oil

perfume

water

dish detergent

✖ Do not taste the liquids

Try adding some of the things you see on this page to water. What do you see? Which ones dissolve? What will happen if you stir the mixtures with a spoon or a hand whisk?

vegetable oil

baking powder

milk

rice

butter

water

vinegar

brown sugar

flour

bath salts

Scientific Principles

Different liquids have different properties; they smell different and flow at different rates. Some solids will dissolve in water. Others are insoluble and will not dissolve. Some liquids will mix with water, others will not. Stirring a solution with a spoon or whisk will aid the process of mixing or dissolving.

Children with asthma may need to be supervised for activities that involve smelling. ✖

Is water always a liquid?

Discover if water can change into a gas or become solid. Ask your child what happens to water when it is heated. Talk about what snow is, or where steam comes from.

What will happen if you leave water in a freezer overnight?

Leave a bottle in a fridge for an hour. What happens to the outside of the bottle when you take it out of the fridge?

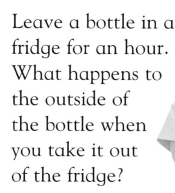

Leave some water in a warm place for two days. What happens?

Scientific Principles

Water can exist in different states; solid (ice), liquid (water), and gas (water vapor). It can change from one state to another through the processes of freezing, melting, condensation, and evaporation. Water vapor in the air condenses into water droplets on the cold bottle. This shows water changing from a gas to a liquid. When water is left in a warm place it evaporates, changing from a liquid to a gas.

What happens when you leave ice out of the freezer?

✗ Wear gloves when handling blocks of ice.

What shape is water?

Investigate the shape of water and test what happens when water is dropped onto different materials. Ask your child to predict the results of the experiments. Help him to make a record of the results of the drip race.

Fill a plastic bag with water. How can you change its shape?

Have a drip race by putting drops of water, dish detergent, and vegetable oil on a mirror. Which liquid will run down the mirror the fastest?

Put a drop of water on different kinds of materials. What happens? Which material would be the best for mopping up a spilled drink?

Can you make drops of water hang from your fingers? What shape are the drops?

Scientific Principles

Water flows, spreads, and forms drops. Water drops "cling" to some surfaces. Some materials absorb water.

kitchen towel

toilet paper

plastic   aluminum foil   velvet

Can you fill it with water?

Experiment with pouring water and filling containers. Ask which containers will hold the most water, and talk about which shapes are easiest to fill. Encourage your child to observe what happens to the water when it is being poured and when it is still.

Use a jug of water to fill some bottles. How many jugs of water does it take to fill each bottle?

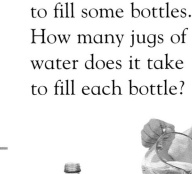

Put some empty plastic bottles into water. What happens? Which one fills up the fastest?

Make some holes like these in plastic bottles. Fill each bottle with water. Which bottle empties the fastest?

💡 Scientific Principles

Liquids can be poured, fill a container, and form a level surface when still. Filling and emptying containers will help children learn about capacity—i.e., how much a container will hold.

Can you move water?

Try these different ways of moving water. Help your child to make a chart to show the easiest ways of moving water. Ask your child which thing would be best for moving a small amount of water or for a large amount of water.

How can you move water using a drinking straw?

Is it easier to move water with one hand or two hands?

Can you move water using a spoon? What happens if you use a sieve?

Scientific Principles

These experiments show that it is easy to move water and that a variety of implements can be used. Water can flow, be held in containers, poured, sucked, or squirted.

Fill a tube with water. Use a funnel to help you. What happens if you lift one end of the tube?

Can you move water using a squeeze bottle or a spray bottle?

Will it float on water?

Try these experiments to discover what things will float on water and what things will sink. Ask your child to find some different things to drop into water and try to guess which ones will float.

Hold a table-tennis ball under water. What does it feel like? What happens when you let go of the ball?

What will happen when you drop your things into water? Do they float?

Scientific Principles

All solid objects are pulled down by the force of gravity. Water exerts an upward force on an object, causing it to float. When the pull of gravity is greater than the upward forces exerted by water, the object sinks. When holding a table-tennis ball under water, children will feel an upward force trying to make the ball float.

How many ways can you find to make a plastic bowl sink?

Will it move in water?

Try these activities to find out which things move through water easily. Talk about how well things such as fish, ducks, or boats move through water. Discuss the shape of each thing. Ask your child what it feels like to wade through water. Ask if it is easier when wearing rubber boots.

Try making different objects move through water. Experiment with different ways of making them move, such as fanning, blowing, or splashing. Which things move through water the fastest?

Make a sailing boat using paper, a plastic tray, modeling clay, and a small stick. Which shape of sail makes your boat go the fastest? Are two sails better than one?

Scientific Principles

As an object moves through water, the water resistance acts to slow it down. Some shapes are better at overcoming water resistance and move more easily.
The shape of a sail will affect how well a boat moves through water. The boats will sail faster with two sails.

Children with asthma may need to be supervised for blowing activities.

Air and Flying

These experiments challenge children to detect the presence of air and to investigate its physical properties. The activities lead children to explore how different shapes fall or fly in the air, how air can be moved, and how moving air can be used to propel objects.

Children can discover that:

AIR IS ALL AROUND US and although we cannot see, taste, or smell it, we can feel it.

AIR HAS MASS and moves to fill spaces.

FORCES CAN MOVE AIR, and the movement can be detected as wind.

WHEN AIR IS HEATED, it will expand and when it is cooled it will contract.

AIR RESISTANCE slows objects down, but some shapes are better at overcoming air resistance than others.

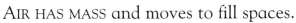

AIR CAN BE POLLUTED, and some forms of pollution can be seen. Clean air is essential to life.

Can you feel the air?

Try these different ways of detecting the presence of air. Ask your child if he can see, feel, taste, or hear the air in each experiment.

What do you feel when you wave your hand? What will happen if you put a paper bag over one hand and wave again?

What happens when you squeeze a plastic bottle filled with air? Does it feel the same with the top open?

Scientific Principles

Air is all around us. Although we cannot see, smell, or taste it, its presence can be detected by feeling it against our bodies or by observing its effect on other objects, e.g., a streamer on a windy day. The paper bag makes a large surface against which air resistance can be felt. Squeezing an empty dish detergent bottle shows air can be squashed.

What does air escaping from a balloon sound like? What does it feel like? Which part of your body feels the moving air the best?

What will air do to a streamer on a windy day?

What is air like?

Find out more about air. Discover if air is heavy and if it is affected by heat. Ask about different ways of finding out how heavy things are. Talk about how hot air can be used—for example, in a hot-air balloon.

Hang a stick from a string. Tape two balloons to the stick and make it balance. Blow up one of the balloons and tape it back on the stick in the same place. What happens?

Cut out a paper snake like this and tape it to a cotton thread.

Blow up two balloons to the same size. Put one balloon in the fridge and the other in a warm place for a few hours. What happens to the balloons?

What will happen when you hold the snake over a lamp?

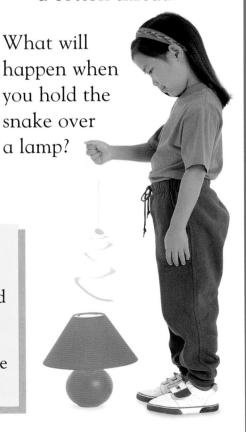

Scientific Principles

Each of these experiments demonstrates a different physical property of air. Balancing two deflated balloons and then inflating one of them shows that air has mass. Putting balloons in warm and cold places shows that air expands when it is hot and contracts when it is cold. The paper snake activity shows that warm air moves upward.

Children with asthma may need to be supervised for blowing activities.

Where is the air?

Try these different experiments to capture the air. Ask your child where the air is in each of the activities.

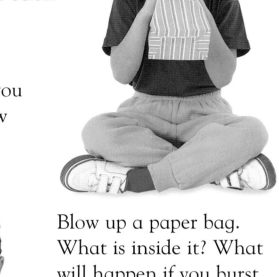

What do you see if you blow through a straw into some water?

Blow up a paper bag. What is inside it? What will happen if you burst the bag with your hands?

What do you see when you put a brick into water? What happens when you put a bottle without a top into water?

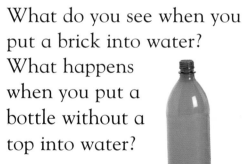

Scientific Principles

Although air is invisible, it exists. It can be blown into bubbles in water or into a paper bag. It can be trapped in soap solution and will escape from an object in the form of bubbles if the object is put in water.

Can you trap air in soap bubbles? Mix some liquid dish detergent with water and dip a loop of rope into it.

Children with asthma may need to be supervised for blowing activities.

Can you make air move?

Investigate the effects of making air move in different ways. Experiment with blowing, pumping, and sucking. Talk to your child about machines that make air move—for example, vacuum cleaners or hair dryers.

How quickly can you pump air into a balloon? What happens to the balloon?

How can you move large beads with a straw? What happens if you prick a hole in the straw?

Hang a table-tennis ball on a string in front of you. Blow through a straw. How do you know if the air is moving?

Scientific Principles

Blowing air against objects applies a force on them and can make them move. Sucking or blowing air through a straw will pull or push an object in the direction of the air flow.

Will it stay in the air?

Find out what kinds of things you can keep up in the air. Talk about how things such as butterflies, bees, or dandelion seeds stay up in the air. Ask your child if some things stay up in the air more easily than others.

How can you keep a feather in the air? How high can you make it go?

For how long can you keep a balloon in the air?

Scientific Principles

An object falling through the air encounters air resistance, which slows its rate of descent. An object with a large surface area has more contact with the air and falls more slowly. The sheet of paper, balloon, and feather are easier to keep up in the air since they have large surface areas and fall slowly. The crumpled sheet of paper has a small surface area and falls more quickly.

Will a sheet of paper stay in the air for longer than a crumpled-up one?

Children with asthma may need to be supervised for blowing activities.

Will it fly or fall?

Discover if things fly or fall when you throw them up in the air, and find ways of making them fall more slowly. Talk about how things such as leaves, sycamore seeds, or raindrops fall.

Make a feather cork by pushing feathers into a cork. What happens when you throw the cork up in the air? What will happen if you add more feathers?

Make a parachute like this with a square of cloth.

cloth

tape

small toy

string

Will it fall faster if you use a bigger piece of cloth?

Make boomerangs like these from stiff cardboard. Flick them into the air with your fingers. Which shape flies best?

Scientific Principle

An object can be made to fall more slowly by making its surface area larger. Adding more feathers to the cork or using a bigger parachute for the toy increases their surface area, causing them to fall more slowly. Objects fly in different ways. The shapes of the boomerangs make them turn in the air. They spin around their center of gravity as they fly.

Will air make it move?

Find out how moving air can make objects move. Talk about what makes a boat move or a weather vane spin. Ask what happens to fallen leaves or a hat on a windy day.

What happens when you blow on a windmill? What happens when you blow hard? What happens when you blow softly?

Cut a slit in the side of a plastic pot. Blow up a balloon and pull the open end through the slit. What happens when you float your balloon boat on water?

Make a blow rocket. How far can you make it go? Will it fly better with paper wings?

modeling clay

thick straw

thin straw

Scientific Principles

Moving air provides the force to propel objects. The blow rocket and windmill are propelled by blowing. The blow rocket will fly better with wings because they give it greater lift and stability. The boats are driven by pushing. Air escaping from the balloons pushes against the surrounding air.

Children with asthma may need to be supervised for blowing activities.

Is the air clean?

Discover what things need clean air. Find out if the air where you live is clean. Talk about why we breathe. Ask your child if she can hold her breath or if it is pleasant to breathe smoky air.

Can you see any birds in the sky? How do they move in the air? Which other living things can fly?

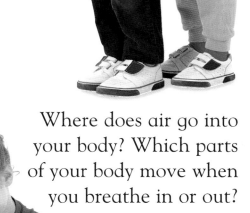

Where does air go into your body? Which parts of your body move when you breathe in or out?

Scientific Principles

Air is essential to living things since it contains gases that support life. Many creatures use the air. All creatures need air to breathe. Air can be polluted and some forms of pollution can be seen. Leaving a sheet of paper outside will reveal that there are dirt and dust particles in the air.

Spread a sheet of paper outside and leave some things on it for a few days. What will you see when you go back and lift up the things?

Children with asthma will need to be supervised when holding their breath.

Make it Change

These activities enable children to experiment with a range of everyday materials and substances and to find ways to make them change, including heating, cooling, stirring, staining, and soaking. They will observe that changes can happen quickly or slowly, and that some changes are irreversible.

Children will discover that:

SOME SUBSTANCES, e.g., sugar, will dissolve in water to form a solution, and that this process can be aided by heating or stirring.

WHEN A LIQUID freezes, it can become a solid. For example, water becomes ice.

WHEN SOME SOLIDS are heated they can become liquid. For example, chocolate melts.

ORGANIC MATTER will decay if left for a period of time. For example, bread will grow moldy.

WET THINGS BECOME DRY when water evaporates. For example, wet clothes dry on a clothesline.

Does it change?

These experiments produce changes that your child can see or feel. Encourage your child to predict the results of the experiments. In each activity ask if things are hot or cold, or solid or liquid.

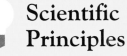

What happens to an ice-cream pop when you suck it? How does your tongue feel?

Rub your hands together very quickly. What happens to your hands?

How does butter change when you hold it?

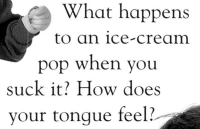

Scientific Principles

Hot hands or mouths will transfer energy into butter, an ice-cream pop, or chocolate and cause them to melt. They change from a solid state to a liquid state. When you rub your hands together quickly, you generate a form of energy called friction. Frictional energy is felt as heat.

Hold some chocolate in your hand. Put some in your mouth. How does the chocolate change?

Does it change in water?

Find out what happens to different solids and liquids when you put them in water. Do they stay the same or do they change?

Try putting some of these things in water. What changes can you see? What happens if you stir the water?

powdered detergent

flour

salt

pasta

coffee

sugar

vegetable oil

toothpaste

Try adding these things to cold water. What happens? Now drop them into warm water. How do they change?

ice

tea bag

butter

28

Can you stir it?

Discover if things change when you stir or shake them. Talk to your child about ways of stirring things— for instance, with a wooden spoon or fork. Ask what he would stir with each utensil.

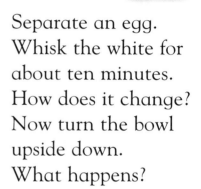

Add a little milk to cornstarch. Is it easy to stir? Leave the cornstarch for about five minutes. How easy is it to stir now?

Separate an egg. Whisk the white for about ten minutes. How does it change? Now turn the bowl upside down. What happens?

Pour some cream into a clean jar and screw on the lid. Shake it for about ten minutes. What happens?

What happens when you turn a bottle of ketchup upside down? Now try again, but shake the bottle first. Is there any change?

Scientific Principles

The properties of some materials can be made to change when energy is applied to them by stirring or shaking. For instance, the white of an egg becomes firm, cream turns to solid butter, and ketchup becomes runny.

Can you cook it?

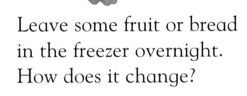

Find out what happens to food when you heat or cool it. Talk to your child about different ways of cooking food—for example, baking cakes or toasting bread. Ask her how the food changes and if it can change back again.

Crack open a raw egg. What is it like inside? Ask an adult to boil an egg. When the egg has cooled, break it open. How has it changed?

Leave some fruit or bread in the freezer overnight. How does it change?

What happens to ice cream when you leave it out of the freezer?

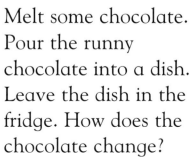

Melt some chocolate. Pour the runny chocolate into a dish. Leave the dish in the fridge. How does the chocolate change?

Can you make it wet?

Find out if things stay the same or change when they are wet. Ask your child what it feels like to get wet—for instance, when having a bath, swimming, or walking in the rain.

How do your hands feel when you put them in water?

How does your hair change when you make it wet? What happens when you use a hair dryer on wet hair?

Put some things in water. Which things soak up the most water? Hang the things on the line to dry. Which ones dry first? Do they look or feel different?

Scientific Principles

When some materials are made wet they may absorb water, become larger, or change color. Different materials dry at different rates. As a material dries, its texture may change or it may shrink. Materials dry when water evaporates from the surface.

Can you make it dirty?

Experiment with different ways of making things dirty and then find ways of making them clean. Talk to your child about ways of cleaning, such as washing, brushing, scrubbing, or polishing. Ask what things she would clean in these ways.

How does a rag change if you rub it in mud?

Put a rag into a pan with some water and sliced beets. Ask an adult to boil the rag for 15 minutes. What happens?

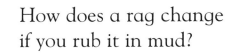

Dip a rag in water dyed with food coloring. How does the rag change?

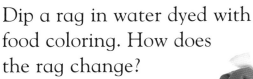

How can you clean the dirty rags? Try washing them in cold water, warm water, and powdered detergent. Which stain is hardest to wash out?

Scientific Principles

Some things will change color when they are made dirty. The stain may be temporary or permanent. Water or detergents will remove some stains.

Will it change?

seeds

Discover if things change when they are left over a period of time. Ask your child to draw each item and to predict what will happen to it. Ask her to draw the item again at the end of the experiment. Talk about the changes that have occurred.

bolts

What will happen to these things if you bury them? If you use a trough, make sure it has holes in the bottom and stand it outside. Water the things you bury and leave them for three or four weeks.

lettuce

Flags showing things you have buried

How do things change when you soak them in water for a long time?

Scientific Principles

If things are left in the soil or water, or are exposed to the air, the process of decay may begin causing the thing to change. For example, non-galvanized bolts will rust if left in the soil, food will grow mold if exposed to the air, dried foods will swell if left in water. Some of these changes may be permanent.

Cover some bread or fruit with plastic wrap. Leave it in a warm place for a few days. What happens?

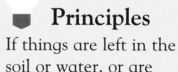

Wear gloves when working with soil.

33

Can you see it change?

Try these experiments and observe the changes that take place. Before each activity ask your child to guess what will happen.

Draw a picture with your finger using lemon juice as ink. Let the lemon juice dry. Ask an adult to iron your picture. How does it change?

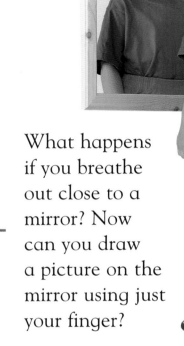

What happens if you breathe out close to a mirror? Now can you draw a picture on the mirror using just your finger?

What happens when you drop a grape into a glass of soda?

Scientific Principles

Here materials are made to change or behave differently. Heat from the iron chars the lemon juice, making it visible. As warm air hits the cold mirror, water vapor in the air condenses, forming water droplets. The grape sinks when it is dropped into the soda. Then, as bubbles stick to its surface, it floats. When the grape hits the surface of the soda, the bubbles burst and it sinks again.

Sound and Music

These experiments encourage children to make and listen to a range of sounds. They discover how to make different sounds, first by using their voices and bodies, and then by using everyday objects and musical instruments, including those they have made themselves.

Children can discover that:

SOUNDS ARE CREATED by making objects vibrate—for example, when they are plucked, beaten, shaken, scraped, banged, or blown.

THE PITCH OF A SOUND can be changed by making an object vibrate at different speeds.

THE QUALITY, OR TIMBRE, of a sound depends on the material from which the instrument is made and the way it is played.

WE HEAR SOUNDS with our ears.

SOUND CAN TRAVEL through different materials. Some materials can prevent sound from passing through.

Can you make sounds?

Try these activities to make sounds using your voice and body. Encourage your child to make as many different sounds as possible. Try whistling, popping, patting, tapping, and scratching. Ask him to combine the sounds. Which is the best sound?

Can you sing a song? How softly can you sing it? Try humming a tune. How loudly can you hum?

Stamp your feet. Make up a beat. Can you click your fingers? Can you click your fingers and stamp your feet at the same time?

How loudly can you shout to a friend?

Scientific Principles

Sounds are caused by vibrations that are carried through the air or other media. The eardrum vibrates when it picks up sound waves and sends messages to the brain that are interpreted as sound.

Clap hands with a friend. How quickly can you clap? How slowly can you clap? Do you know a clapping song? Can you clap in time to the song?

Can you twang, pluck, or flap it?

Explore these different ways to make sounds. Ask your child if the sounds are high or low. Experiment with different materials—for example, try a metal ruler, sheets of aluminum foil, or string. Are the sounds the same?

What sound does cardboard make when you flap it?

Stretch an elastic band around a chair. Does it make a sound when you pluck it? What happens when you pull harder?

Hold a ruler on the seat of a chair. Press down one end of the ruler and then let go. Does it make a sound?

Make a guitar box with thick and thin elastic bands and a box. Which type of band makes a low sound when you pluck it?

Scientific Principles

When an object vibrates, it makes a sound. Different objects vibrate at different rates and produce sounds of different pitch. An object that vibrates quickly will produce a high-pitched sound. An object that vibrates slowly will produce a low-pitched sound.

Can you tap or bang it?

Experiment with tapping and banging different materials. Try wood, metal, glass, plastic, and pottery. Are the sounds different? Talk to your child about how to make loud and soft sounds. Ask her to predict which object will make the loudest sound.

Can you make sounds by banging? Try saucepan lids, plastic bowls, or spoons. Which sound do you like best?

Make different sounds by tapping. Start by tapping with your fingers. Try tapping with different beaters. Does a wooden spoon make the same sound as a metal spoon?

Make a chime by hanging things on a coat hanger. Can you tap out a tune? What makes a high sound?

Scientific Principles

The quality, or timbre, of a sound depends on the material that is making the sound. For instance, wood makes a different type of sound than metal.

Can you shake or scrape it?

Try making these different shakers with pots, plastic bottles, and cups. Put things such as beads, rice, or corks in the shakers, and compare the sounds they make. Ask your child if the shakers make high or low sounds.

Put different things into containers and shake them. Which shaker makes the best sound?

Make this rattle. Thread various things onto a length of string. Tape the string to a stick. What happens when you shake the stick? How will it sound if you thread only buttons or bottle caps onto the string?

Scientific Principles

The speed at which the binding is scraped will affect the pitch of the sound. The binding will make a higher sound if the spirals are scraped quickly and a lower sound if scraped slowly.

Use a spoon to scrape the spiral binding of a notebook. What happens when you scrape slowly?

 You may wish to supervise when your child makes the rattle.

Can you blow it?

Experiment with using your breath to make sounds. Talk to your child about wind instruments, such as a recorder, flute, or trumpet. Ask how the instruments are played.

Make a reed pipe with a large paper straw. Flatten one end of the straw and cut it to a point. Blow through the pointed end. What kind of sound does the straw make?

What happens to the sound when you cut the straw in half?

How can you make a very loud sound with a whistle?

Try blowing softly over the neck of some bottles. Does a large bottle make the same sound as a small bottle?

Scientific Principles

Sound can be produced by making air vibrate. A large bottle will make a lower sound than a small bottle. Altering the length of a column of air— for example, cutting the reed pipe in half—will produce notes of different pitch. The volume can be controlled by blowing hard or gently.

Children with asthma may need to be supervised for blowing activities.

Is the sound loud or soft?

Find out about volume. Ask your child to do something as loudly as possible, such as stamp or clap. Then to do something very quietly, such as whisper or tiptoe.

How can you make a loud sound with a drum?

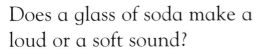

Does a glass of soda make a loud or a soft sound?

Try listening to different sounds such as paper rustling, or a radio playing. Ask your friend to make the sounds for you.

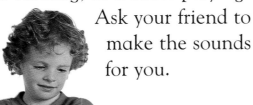

Can you stop yourself from hearing the sounds? Cover your ears with your hands or with some cotton balls. Which works best?

Scientific Principles

We can distinguish between soft and loud sounds. The loudness of a sound depends on the size of the vibration making the sound. The larger the vibration, the louder the sound. Sound does not travel well through all materials, e.g., cotton balls. Materials that do not transmit sounds well can be used for soundproofing.

Can you hear through things?

Discover if sound can travel through things. Ask your child if it is always easy to hear what someone says, for instance, when in another room, or on opposite sides of the window, or under water.

Can you hear a watch ticking through a balloon? What happens if you fill the balloon with water?

What can you hear if you put your ear to the ground?

Make a string telephone by threading a length of string through two plastic cups. Use two buttons to hold the cups in place at each end of the string.

Scientific Principles

Sound can travel through different materials. Some materials, for example, wire, carry sounds better than others.

Can you hear through the telephone? Can you hear around a corner? What happens if you use thin wire?

Can you feel it moving?

Try these activities to find out if things move when they make a sound. Ask your child if things such as metal trash cans, saucepan lids, or bottles move when they are hit. Ask which things make a sound.

Put your fingers on your neck. What can you feel when you talk, sing, or shout loudly?

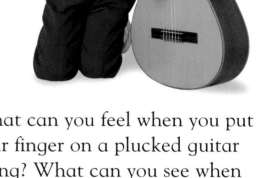

Make a kazoo with a comb and some tissue paper. Fold the paper around the comb. Put your lips to the paper and hum a tune. How do your lips feel?

What can you feel when you put your finger on a plucked guitar string? What can you see when you pluck the string?

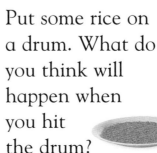

Scientific Principles

When an object moves back and forth quickly, e.g., a plucked guitar string, it is said to vibrate. We can see, feel, and hear these vibrations.

Put some rice on a drum. What do you think will happen when you hit the drum?

43

Color and Light

These experiments encourage young children to investigate the concepts of light and dark, shadow and reflection, the color spectrum, and camouflage. Children are challenged to make light bounce, to create shadows, and to mix and match colors.

Children can discover that:

OUR EYES ENABLE US to see light coming from different sources, and we see objects because they give out or reflect light.

LIGHT CAN BE SEEN through materials to varying degrees, and some materials stop light altogether.

WHITE LIGHT FROM THE SUN is a combination of all the colors of the rainbow. When light passes through transparent materials, e.g., water or glass, the rays are bent or refracted as they go through.

WHEN LIGHT RAYS hit a shiny surface, they are reflected.

What can you see?

Try these activities to explore light and dark. Ask your child if it is easier to do things with one eye closed. Talk about different light sources—sunshine, light bulbs, flashlights, headlights, television screens, and night-lights.

Close your eyes and cover them. What colors can you see? Can you tell when a flashlight is on?

Make a cave with a blanket and some chairs or boxes. How can you make it really dark inside?

Scientific Principles

Light is emitted from sources such as the Sun, flashlights, and electric lights. These activities show that light is necessary to see.

Sit inside your cave. What can you see in the dark? How many different ways can you think of to make it light inside your cave?

Can you see through it?

Discover if light passes through all materials. Talk to your child about things that are used to vary the brightness of light—for example, sunglasses, tinted windows, and lampshades.

Do you think you can see light though your hand?

Collect lots of different objects. Can you find things made of plastic, metal, glass, fabric, china, and wood? What do you see when you shine a flashlight on them?

Look through a sheet of colored plastic. What do you see?

Scientific Principles

Light does not go through all materials. Some materials are transparent, which means they let light through (clear glass), some materials are translucent and let some light through (frosted glass), and some materials are opaque, which means they completely stop light (wood).

Can you shine a flashlight close to things? What sort of objects does the light shine through?

Can you make shadows?

Play these games with your child to make shadows outside and inside. Talk about how you can change the size and shape of a shadow.

Try to find your shadow on a sunny day. Is it always the same shape and size?

Make a paper fish with a straw handle. Shine a flashlight on the fish. Try to make fish shadows swim across the wall. What happens when you hold the flashlight closer to the fish?

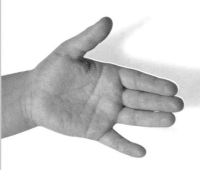

How can you make a shadow that looks like a dog's head? Can you make a butterfly shadow?

Scientific Principles

Shadows form when a beam of light is interrupted—for example, when you stand between the sun and a light-colored surface. The shape and size of a shadow depend on how far the object is from the light source. The closer the object is to the light, the bigger the shadow will be.

Put a sheet of paper on the wall. Ask a friend to make a head shadow. Can you draw around the shadow of your friend's head?

Can you see yourself?

Try these activities with mirrors and shiny objects to find out how light can be reflected. Ask your child to look for different places she might see her reflection—for instance, in puddles, aluminum foil, or a saucepan.

Find some shiny objects. What do you see when you look at them?

What do you see when you look into a bowl of water? What will happen if you put your finger in the water?

Look into a bending plastic mirror. What happens to your face?

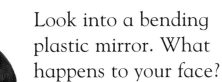

Scientific Principles

When light rays hit a shiny surface, such as a mirror, they bounce off, or "reflect." A bending mirror or rippled water will distort the reflection. Flat mirrors produce an image the same size as the object, but left and right are reversed.

Can you look into a mirror and touch your nose?

What can mirrors do?

Discover how mirrors can be used to bounce light and to see around corners. Talk about the practical ways in which mirrors and reflective surfaces are used— for instance, rearview mirrors in cars, a dentist's mirror, and reflectors on bicycles.

How can you make light bounce onto the ceiling using a small mirror and a flashlight?

What will happen to a light beam if you shine it through a magnifying glass onto a wall?

Shine a flashlight onto a mirror through a tube. Will you be able to make the light turn a corner and catch it in another tube?

Scientific Principles

Light travels in straight lines. When it strikes a mirror, it is reflected off the surface at the same angle that it comes in at. Light will bounce off a mirror onto the ceiling if you angle the mirror upward. When light rays pass though a magnifying glass they are focused onto one spot.

Can you see colors?

Play these games to find the colors in light. Look for a rainbow when there is sunshine and rain, or draw a picture together showing the colors in a rainbow—red, orange, yellow, green, blue, indigo, and violet.

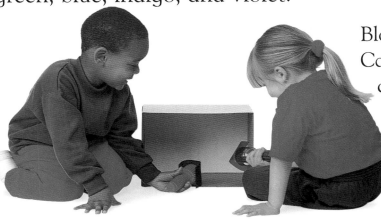

Blow lots of bubbles. Can you see more colors when you are inside or outside?

Cover one flashlight with blue cellophane and one flashlight with red. Shine both flashlights onto the same spot in a white box. Which color will you see?

What can you see when you look through a prism?

Put a bowl of water in sunlight. Add some drops of motor oil. What do you see?

Scientific Principles

Light from the Sun is a combination of seven colors. When light passes through a prism, it is refracted (bent) and split into seven colors. A thin film of oil on water will refract light. Colored lights can be mixed to form new colors.

Can you hide or match it?

Discover how you can use paint and colors to hide things. Talk about the ways animals use color to camouflage themselves.

Ask a friend to stand a long way from you and hold up a picture. Which colors show up best from far away? Which colors do not show up well?

Put your hand on some striped paper. Can you hide your hand against the paper with paint?

Cut out some paper animals. How could you make or paint a background scene to hide them?

Make a picture of a friend. Try to match the color of your friend's hair and eyes.

Scientific Principles

Many animals survive by blending in with their surroundings. This is called camouflage. Camouflage includes color, shape, and patterning. A chameleon changes color to match its surroundings.

Can you make colors?

Try these painting activities with your child to discover what happens when colors are mixed and separated. Look at the shades of color in leaves, pebbles, feathers, and wood.

Can you paint a picture using lots of colors?

How many shades of red can you make with paint? Does adding water change the color?

Scientific Principles

There is a vast range of colors. Mixing and diluting paint colors begins to show this. Separating the colors in paint or ink is called chromatography. It shows which colors have been used to create a colored ink, e.g., purple ink separates into three different colors—black, blue, and red.

Cut coffee-filter paper into strips. Put a blob of ink near one end of a strip with a felt-tipped pen. Let the stain dry, then hold the paper so that it just dips into some water. What happens as the water travels up the paper?

Me and My Body

The following experiments examine different parts of the body. They will show that each part of the body has a job to do. Children will begin to understand that all of us are different in some ways and similar in others.

Children can discover that:

THE HUMAN BODY is made up of parts or organs. Each organ performs a different function.

ALL HUMANS VARY in terms of physical features and abilities. It is important to know that there is no right or wrong way to look.

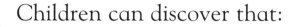

OUR SENSES help us explore our environment. Eyes sense light; ears detect sound; the tongue and nose sense taste and smell; the skin senses texture, heat, and pain.

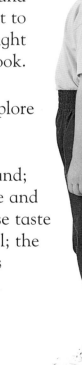

What are you like?

Try these experiments to find out about the external features of the body. Ask your child to name different parts of the body. Talk about whether your child resembles anyone else in the family or if she looks like any of her friends.

How many fingers do you have? Can you make a handprint? What do your fingerprints look like?

What is your skin like?
Is your neck long or short? What is your hair like?

How long are your legs? Can you take a big step? How wide can you stretch your arms?

Scientific Principles

Humans are different from one another. Even identical twins are different. No two humans are identical.

Where is your chest?
Are your shoulders
hard or soft?

What can you do?

Discover what the different parts of your body can do, e.g., bones, muscles, and joints. Encourage your child to find muscles by flexing a fist, opening and shutting his eyes, bending, and hopping.

Where do you have muscles? What do they feel like? What do your bones feel like? Can you feel and draw the bones in your hands?

Can you feel the bones in a friend's back?

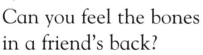

Scientific Principles

Bones make up a strong, flexible framework called a skeleton. Where two bones meet, they form a joint. Joints allow you to move and bend. Muscles are joined to bones. When muscles contract, they make bones move so that you can walk, talk, jump, and bend.

Can you bend and straighten your elbows and knees? Where else does your body bend?

How big are you?

Play these games with your child and her friends to find out who is the biggest. Suggest keeping a record of your child's height every month.

Are you the same height as any of your friends?

Who is your tallest friend?

How heavy are you?
Who is your heaviest friend?
Who is the lightest?

How do you breathe?

Explore the way we breathe and discover what happens to the body when we breathe in and out. Suggest that your child listen to his friend's heartbeat before and after the friend has been active. Does the heartbeat sound different?

Take a deep breath in. Then breathe out slowly. Which part of your body moves? Where do you think your lungs are?

For how long can you blow down a straw into a glass of water?

What happens to your breathing when you run, skip, or jump?

💡 Scientific Principles

Your lungs are in your chest, protected by your ribcage. When you breathe in, air is sucked down into your lungs. When you breathe out, the air that has been used is forced out.

Blow at a paper ball through a straw. How far does the ball move? What will happen if you blow harder?

✗ Children with asthma need to be supervised when blowing through a straw.

What can you feel?

Try these experiments with your child to find out about the sense of touch. Talk about how textures feel on different parts of the body— for example, fingertips, toes, and back.

Cover your eyes. Ask a friend to pass different things to you. Can you guess what the things are by feeling them with your hands?

Can you say what the things are by feeling them with your feet?—

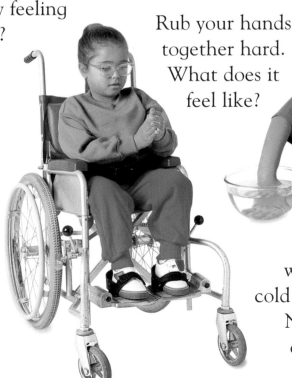

Rub your hands together hard. What does it feel like?

Put one hand into very warm water and one into cold water. Count to twenty. Now put both hands into cool water. How do your hands feel?

What do you see?

Explore the sense of sight. How does it help us to understand the world around us? Discuss why some people cannot see or need to wear glasses.

Talk about the things we use our eyes for, such as reading, writing, and recognizing faces.

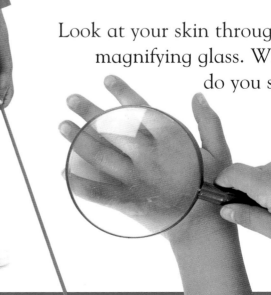

Can you find your way around a room by looking into a mirror like this?

Look at your friend's eyes. What do they look like? Can you see a black hole in the middle of your friend's eye?

Try to find your way around a room blindfolded. Does it help to use a stick?

Look at your skin through a magnifying glass. What do you see?

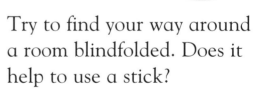

Scientific Principles

You use your eyes to see. The black hole in the middle of the eye is called the pupil. Light enters the eye through the pupil. The coloured part of the eye is called the iris.

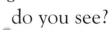

What can you hear?

Play these games to find out about ears and hearing. Talk about all the different sounds you hear around the home. Ask your child if she can make loud and soft noises.

Look at the shape and size of a friend's ear. Use a flashlight to look inside. What can you see?

Cover your ears and walk around a room. Is it easy to walk around if you cannot hear? Try shutting your eyes as well.

Can you guess just by shaking it what a friend has hidden inside a box?

Scientific Principles

The main part of the ear is inside the head. The flappy outer ear you can see acts like a funnel, collecting sounds in the air and sending them into the ear canal. Two ears help you find out better where sound is coming from.

Ask a friend to ring a bell behind you. Can you point to where the sound is coming from? Cover one ear. Can you point to the sound as easily?

What can you taste and smell?

Try these experiments with your child to discover how his mouth and nose work. Ask your child to discuss the tastes and smells he likes and dislikes. Talk about how smells can warn us of danger—for instance, smoke and rotten food.

Look in a mirror. What is your nose like? What do your lips feel like?

Is your tongue rough or smooth?

What do these things taste like when you put them on your tongue?

salt

lemon

sugar

Which things smell nice? Which things have a strong smell? Do you have a favorite smell?

Scientific Principles

The senses of taste and smell work together. The tongue is covered with thousands of tiny taste buds that pick out the tastes in food and drink. You taste salty and sweet things at the end of your tongue and sour food in the middle. Cells inside your nose detect smells.

Can you guess what food you are tasting without seeing it? What happens if you hold your nose as well?

Living Things

These experiments lead children to examine a wide variety of plants and animals and to explore life processes. Children will begin to understand and learn by collecting and observing living things.

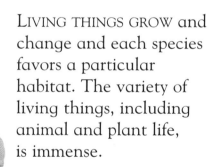

Children can discover that:

BASIC LIFE PROCESSES, such as moving, are common to humans and other animals.

LIVING THINGS GROW and change and each species favors a particular habitat. The variety of living things, including animal and plant life, is immense.

CAREFUL OBSERVATION is required to make comparisons and find similarities and differences among things.

IF ANIMALS ARE TO SURVIVE in the wild or in captivity, we need to consider their welfare and be sensitive to their needs.

What is alive?

Discover what being 'alive' means. Observe things in your home, or outside, and encourage your child to look for signs of life—for instance, does it move, breathe, or grow?

Which of the things shown here are alive? Which things are non living?

Which things were once part of a living thing?
Can you tell which living things they came from?

What things grow and are alive?

What things can you see breathing? Where does the air go in and come out?

What things move and are alive?

Scientific Principles

The criteria of movement, breathing, and growth are used here to judge whether things are living, dead, or have never lived at all.

✗ Wear gloves when handling soil and be careful not to harm living things.

Where do things live?

Try these experiments to determine where living things may be found. Ask your child to think of the kinds of places she would look to find things that are alive.

Cut out pictures of animals that live on a farm and in the wild. Can you make a poster of the animals in their different habitats?

What things live in a park or garden? Do they live in the grass, in trees, in the soil, or under stones?

How many living things can you find in your home?

What things can you find living in a pond?

Scientific Principles

There is a vast variety of living things found in many different habitats. Children can begin to appreciate this by looking at plants and pets in the home, and then considering things in different environments.

Wash your hands after touching pond water and be careful not to fall in!

Can you collect living things?

air holes

rubber band

cover

jar

Examine small creatures more closely by gently collecting some living things. Ask your child to draw pictures of the creatures that he finds.

Find some plastic jars to use for collecting things. Cut out paper covers and fix them in place with rubber bands. How will you care for the animals you collect?

What animals might you catch if you leave a tub in some soil? Balance a cover on two stones, over the tub, to keep the rain out.

Use a net to catch some animals that live in water. Gently put them into a bucket of water.

What do the animals look like?

Scientific Principles

Collecting creatures is the beginning of the process of studying living things in more detail. It is important to remind children to think about each animal's welfare, whether it can breathe and what it will eat.

Can you study living things?

Try these activities to find out about snails and wood lice. Similar experiments can be carried out with earthworms and grasshoppers.

Can you make a home for a snail? Put some stones and damp soil into a tank. Make some air holes in the lid and put something heavy on top to keep the snails from escaping.

Do snails prefer to eat cabbage or lettuce?

What will happen if you gently touch a snail on its head?

Use a magnifying glass to look closely at some animals. Can you draw what you see?

Scientific Principles

Living things need certain conditions to sustain life. These experiments are humane investigations to discover how sensitive mini beasts are to their environment, and what foods they prefer to eat.

Can you find some wood lice? Put them into a box of soil. What will the wood lice do if you cover half of the box?

Wash your hands after touching animals and wear gloves when handling soil.

What are living things like?

Find out more about the external features and characteristics of different plants and animals. Talk about the living things around you, such as pets, bugs, trees, and flowers.

Do all animals have a head? What shapes and colors are their bodies?

How many legs do animals have? Do all animals move in the same way?

What sort of skin do animals have? Is it rough or smooth?

bud

Do all plants have roots, leaves, and a stem?

flower

leaves

stem

roots

How many types of leaves can you find? Can you sort them into groups?

Scientific Principles

Animals are living things that rely on plants or other animals for food. Plants are living things that can make their own food. They are sensitive to environmental changes, but are slow to react.

Are all plants the same?

Discover where fruits and vegetables come from. Talk to your child about where you can find seeds, what they look like, and what they grow into. Explore farther afield in a garden center, supermarket, or park.

Which vegetables and salad foods have leaves? Which vegetables are roots that grow under the ground?

Ask an adult to help you cut some fruits in half. What do they look like inside? Are they all the same?

Scientific Principles

Fruits and vegetables fall into different groups. Fruits produce seeds, which can grow into new plants. Vegetables are plants we eat that do not contain seeds.

Can you collect some seeds from trees and plants? What is the biggest seed you can find?

Children should be warned about the dangers of tasting seeds and berries.

How do living things grow?

Find out how living things grow and change. Look at family photographs and talk about how people change in appearance.

Look at photographs of yourself as a baby. How have you changed? In what ways are you different from an adult?

What will happen if you leave some vegetable tops in a dish of water?

Make a home for a caterpillar. Line a box with damp paper towels and put in some fresh leaves. Gently pick up a caterpillar with a paintbrush and place it in the caterpillar home. Cover the box with muslin. Feed your caterpillar with fresh leaves every day.

How has the caterpillar changed after a few weeks?

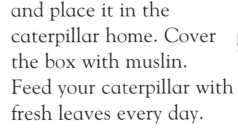

Scientific Principles

All living things grow as the result of using the food they eat or make. Plants and animals grow at different rates and sometimes change in their appearance. Plants need growth to "move" toward the light and gravity.

Avoid species of caterpillar with long hairs since they may cause an allergic irritation.

Are all living things the same?

owls

Look at the creatures on this page. Discuss the ways they are different and the ways they are the same.

Mammals
These animals are known as mammals. Do all mammals have fur?

piglets

dog

human

Birds
How many different birds can you see at the park? Do all birds have feathers?

duck

sparrow

Fish
Do all fish have fins and a tail?

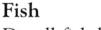
trout

goldfish

shark

Reptiles
What is a reptile's skin like?

frog

lizard

crocodile

snake

Insects
How many legs do insects have?

wasp

beetle

stick insect

ladybug

Scientific Principles
Each group of animals is different from others. Animals are put into groups according to the similarities they share.

Seasons and Weather

In these experiments children will learn progressively about seasons, weather, and simple astronomy. They are encouraged to observe and record daily and seasonal variations in the weather. Other activities lead children to explore temperature changes and the effect of weather on the environment.

Children can discover that:

WEATHER CHANGES ALL THE TIME and these changes can be detected, measured, and recorded.

EXTREMES OF WEATHER have an effect on buildings and rocks.

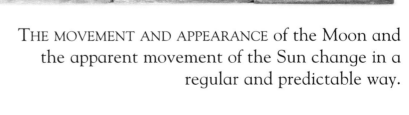

THE MOVEMENT AND APPEARANCE of the Moon and the apparent movement of the Sun change in a regular and predictable way.

THE APPEARANCE of plants and trees and the hours of daylight all change from season to season.

What season is it?

Play these games to discover if it is spring, summer, fall, or winter. Talk about the clothes you wear at different times of the year. Ask your child if it is always dark when she goes to bed and always light when she wakes up.

Look at this tree at different times of the year. What season is it now?

Look outside. What colors can you see? What do the trees look like? What clothes are people wearing?

Scientific Principles

The Earth rotates around the Sun every 365 days. For six months of the year one side of the Earth leans toward the Sun and for six months the other side leans toward the Sun. The side leaning toward the Sun has long, hot days; it is summer. The side leaning away has short days; it is winter.

Try dressing up for different seasons and weather. What do you put on in the summer if it is hot? What do you wear when it is cold in the winter? What things do you need in wet weather?

Is the Sun or the Moon out?

Try these experiments to find out about the Sun and the Moon. Remind your child to never look directly at the Sun.

Cut out some circles of paper to look like the Sun.

Stick a paper Sun onto the window where you can see the real Sun. Do this at different times of the day. Is the Sun always in the same place?

Where is the Sun in the morning?

Where is the Sun at noon?

Where is the Sun in the afternoon?

When can you see the Moon? Is it always in the same place? Does it look like any of these shapes?

new Moon	crescent Moon	half Moon	gibbous Moon	full Moon	gibbous Moon	half Moon	crescent Moon

Scientific Principles

The Earth rotates on its axis once every 24 hours. The Earth orbits around the Sun. Seen from the Earth, the Sun appears to rise in the east and set in the west. The Moon orbits around the Earth every 28 days. The Moon is illuminated to different degrees during the lunar month by the light of the Sun. These differences in the Moon's appearance are shown in the above illustration.

Is it cloudy or rainy today?

Find out about clouds and rain. Ask your child to draw some differently shaped clouds. Talk about where rain comes from and what clouds look like on a wet day.

Put some sticky tape on a window where you can see a cloud. After one minute, mark the cloud again. Is the cloud moving quickly or slowly? What makes the cloud move?

| storm clouds | rain clouds | high clouds | clear sky |

Can you see clouds in the sky today? Do they look like any of these clouds? Do you think it will rain today?

Go outside on a rainy day. Does the rain soak a sheet of paper slowly or quickly?

Scientific Principles

Clouds are made up of water in its vapor and/or water state. Cloud conditions can be used to predict the weather. Rain results when water in the atmosphere cools from its vapor state into its liquid state.

How hot is it?

Discover the temperature of different things. Talk about the clothes you wear to make you feel warm and the clothes you wear to feel cool.

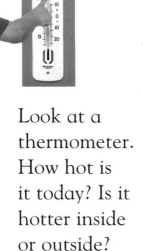

Look at a thermometer. How hot is it today? Is it hotter inside or outside?

Put some warm water in a glass. How can you find out how warm the water is?

Put a strip thermometer on your forehead. How hot are you?

Wrap your hand in different types of fabric. Which fabric makes your hand feel hottest? Which fabric feels coolest?

muslin / wool / polyester \ cotton

Scientific Principles

Temperature is measured in degrees Celsius or Fahrenheit. A thermometer measures how hot things are. The more air trapped in a fabric—e.g., wool, the warmer it feels.

Does it stay hot or cold?

Discover how things stay hot and how to keep things cold. Discuss the ways you keep drinks cold and feet warm.

What happens when you pour water onto ice or snow? What will happen if you leave ice or snow indoors?

Have you ever seen snow? What does it feel like? Does snow have a smell? Can you make a snowball?

Leave some ice cubes in a bowl and wrap some others in aluminum foil. What happens to the ice cubes?

Which wrapping will keep a hot-water bottle warm for the longest time?

aluminum foil

blanket

newspaper

Scientific Principles

Some materials, such as foil, are good thermal conductors, which means they carry heat away from something. Poor conductors are called insulators. Air trapped in the fibers of a blanket is a good insulator and slows down heat loss.

How windy is it today?

Find out how windy it is with these fun experiments. Talk about what wind feels like, and how it makes things move.

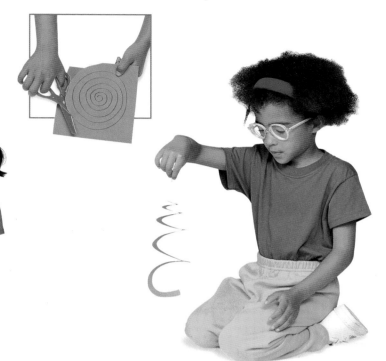

Go outside on a windy day. Wet your finger and hold it up in the air. How can you tell which way the wind is blowing?

Draw a spiral on a piece of card. Cut it out to make a snake. Tape a piece of thread to the snake. What happens when you hold the snake in the wind?

Hang cardboard of different thicknesses from a broom handle. What will happen when the wind blows gently? What happens when it blows strongly?

Scientific Principles

Wind is the movement of the air from hot areas to cooler ones. The force of the wind can be seen by hanging cardboard of different thicknesses in the changing wind.
The force of the wind will make the wind snake spin faster in strong winds, or slower in gentle winds.

Measuring the weather

Make a wind gauge, a wind vane, and a rain gauge with your child and record the weather conditions every day. Keep a weather diary using weather signs.

Make a wind vane to find out which way the wind is blowing. Draw an arrow on the point of the card. Take your wind vane outside. How will it show you which way the wind is blowing?

curved cardboard

tape

knitting needle

plastic pen case

Make a wind gauge. Tape a curved piece of cardboard to a knitting needle. Put one end into a plastic pen case. Hold your wind gauge in the wind. Does it show you how hard the wind is blowing?

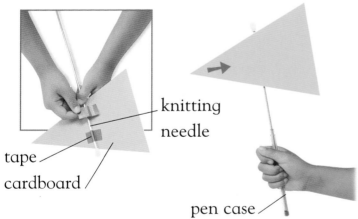

knitting needle

tape

cardboard

pen case

Make a rain gauge. Place a funnel on top of a jar. Tape a ruler to the side of the jar. How can you find out how much rain falls in one week?

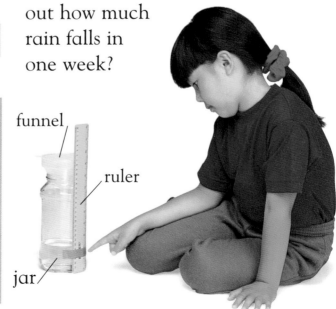

funnel

ruler

jar

Scientific Principles

Weather is the range of atmospheric conditions that exists at a given time. These conditions, e.g.,—rainfall, temperature, wind speed, wind direction, and cloud cover—can be measured. Changes in these conditions can be used to predict future weather.

Can weather change things?

Find out what wind, rain, and ice do to rocks, soil, and buildings. Look at local buildings with your child for signs of erosion.

Find out what rain can do by pouring water onto a pile of stones, soil, or sand. What do you think will happen?

stones

soil

pebbles

sand

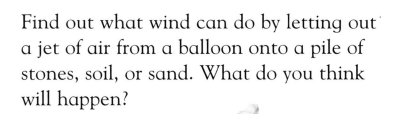

Find out what wind can do by letting out a jet of air from a balloon onto a pile of stones, soil, or sand. What do you think will happen?

Scientific Principles

Over time, rain and wind wear away rock, and move pebbles, soil, and sand. The water in the mud ball will expand as it freezes and the ball will crack. This happens to soil and rocks in icy weather.

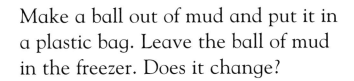

Make a ball out of mud and put it in a plastic bag. Leave the ball of mud in the freezer. Does it change?

Make it Balance

These experiments encourage young children to investigate their own physical ability to balance, and to find ways of balancing a range of objects. Ideas about mass are introduced by asking children to compare heavy and light objects.

Children can discover that:

AN OBJECT HAS a balancing point. This can be directly above or below its center of gravity, also known as the center of mass, where most of an object's mass appears to be concentrated.

AN OBJECT IS SUBJECT to the force of gravity and, in certain circumstances, this force will cause it to topple over.

OBJECTS WITH a low center of gravity – objects that are heavier at the base – tend to be more stable.

TO BALANCE AN object, opposing forces must be balanced by changing the object's position or by lowering its center of gravity.

Can you balance?

Carry out these experiments to explore balance. Ask your child to try balancing in different positions. Talk about which ways of balancing are easy and which are more difficult.

Can you balance on one hand and one foot? How high can you lift your leg and arm?

Can you stand on one leg? Can you balance while you count to ten?

Can you balance on tiptoe?

Scientific Principles

The body's mass is subject to the force of gravity, which pulls it toward the center of the Earth. To balance, children must adjust the position of their bodies so that their center of gravity (also known as center of mass) is directly above the point on which they are balancing.

Can you balance on your head and straighten your legs?

Can you balance on things?

Try balancing on different things without falling off. Talk about what makes it easier to balance. Ask your child to try crouching down on the uneven blocks. Does this make balancing easier? What happens if he closes his eyes?

Can you stand on two things of uneven height? Can you keep your balance?

Can you keep your balance on bucket-stilts?

Can you balance on a low wall and walk along? Try carrying a broom, or plastic bottles filled with water. Does this make a difference?

Scientific Principles

Lowering an object's center of gravity makes it easier to balance. Crouching down on the uneven blocks and on the bucket-stilts lowers the center of gravity, which increases the stability of the child's body, making it easier to balance.

Will it balance?

Ask your child what things can be balanced on different parts of the body. Try to balance a pencil or a spoon on one finger or hand. Why do some things balance more easily than others? Does changing the position of an object help to stop it from toppling over?

Can you balance a cushion on your head?

Can you stand up with a book balanced on your head? Is it easier with your arms folded?

Can you balance a broom on your hand? Now try balancing it on the top of your foot. Which is easier to do?

What can you balance on the soles of your feet? Is it harder if you use one foot?

Scientific Principles

Inanimate objects are also subject to the force of gravity. Adjusting the position of an object to find its balancing point can stop the object from falling over. An object balances when its center of gravity is directly above or below the point on which it is balancing.

Will it topple?

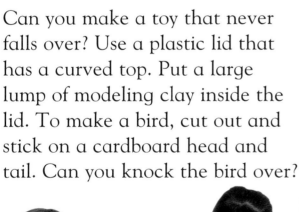

Ask your child to make towers by balancing different things on top of each other. Talk about ways to make the towers more stable. Try making a toppling toy bird. Why does this toy bird never fall over?

Can you build a tower that is taller than you are?

Can you make a toy that never falls over? Use a plastic lid that has a curved top. Put a large lump of modeling clay inside the lid. To make a bird, cut out and stick on a cardboard head and tail. Can you knock the bird over?

Try building a tower with books and plastic cups. How can you make it balance?

Scientific Principles

An object with a broad base is difficult to topple, while one with a narrow base is easy to topple. Widening the base of the tower gives it a lower center of gravity, which makes it more stable. In the toppling toy bird experiment, the modeling clay inside the lid makes the base heavier. This lowers the lid's center of gravity, making it very difficult to knock over.

Does it balance?

Make these cardboard toys and try to get them to balance. Talk about how the position of the modeling clay helps make the toys balance.

Can you make a tightrope walker? Cut a figure out of cardboard. Does it balance on a piece of string?

Now stick lumps of modeling clay onto the figure. Where do you have to put the clay to make the figure balance?

Ask an adult to help you make this dog on a leash. Do you think it will balance on the edge of a table?

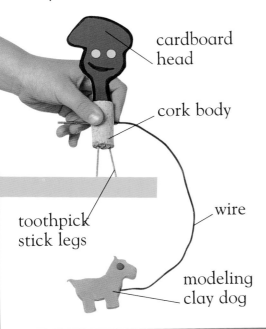

cardboard head

cork body

toothpick stick legs

wire

modeling clay dog

Scientific Principles

A hanging object balances when its center of gravity is directly below its balancing point. In the dog on a leash experiment, the cork's light weight is not important provided that the clay is positioned directly under the cork and cocktail sticks – the balancing point.

Can you feel it balance?

Ask your child if she can balance a tray on one hand. Where does she have to put her hand to feel the tray balance? Try making a mobile from a coat hanger, string, tape, toys, and cardboard cutouts. How can you make heavy toys balance light toys?

Put one plastic cup on the end of a tray. Can you make the tray balance?

Now try two cups. Does the tray balance?

What happens if you add a third cup?

Make a mobile by hanging lengths of string over a coat hanger. Tape a small toy onto each length of string.

What happens if you move the toys to different places on the coat hanger? Can you make the coat hanger balance?

Scientific Principles

A heavy object can be made to balance a lighter object by moving the heavy object nearer to the balancing point and the lighter object farther away. To make a mobile, the correct balancing point for each object has to be found. When a new object is added, the other objects need to be moved.

Will the buckets balance?

Try these experiments to make two buckets balance. Talk about which things are heavy, and which things are light. Your child can also try putting stones, sand, or marbles into the buckets.

Find some different things to balance. Can you tell which things are heavier than others before you put them in a bucket-balance?

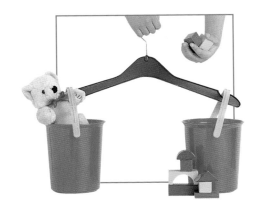

To make a bucket-balance, hook two small buckets onto a coat hanger. Put some of your things into the buckets. What happens when you lift up the bucket-balance?

Fill one bucket with rice and the other with pasta. Which bucket do you think will be heavier?

Scientific Principles

The mass is the amount of material that makes up an object. When equal masses are hung at each end of the coat hanger they will balance. Mass is measured in kilograms and pounds.

Can you make a bucket of water balance a bucket of bananas?

How well can you balance?

Try these activities to see if you are good at balancing!
Ask your child to try balancing in different positions.
Talk about the balancing skills that can be learned, and how these skills help us to balance.

Lean against a wall. Make sure your foot, arm, leg, and one side of your face and body are touching the wall. Can you lift your other leg?

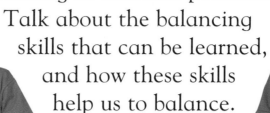

Can you build a tower with playing cards? How many cards can you balance without the tower falling down?

What do you think will happen if you sit on one end of a seesaw and two of your friends sit on the other end?

Scientific Principles

It is impossible to lean against a wall and lift a leg as described in the experiment. Children will find that they cannot keep their center of gravity over their feet without moving their foot away from the wall.

Make it Go

These experiments encourage young children to explore the basic principles associated with movement. By finding various ways to make things go, children begin to learn about forces.

Children can discover that:

OBJECTS MOVE IN A variety of ways. Air, water, and simple machines can be used to make objects move.

FORCES CAN MAKE THINGS MOVE, speed them up, slow them down, and make them stop.

FRICTION IS A FORCE that slows things down. It occurs when two surfaces rub against each other.

FORCES CAN work at a distance. For instance, some metal objects can be moved using a magnetic force.

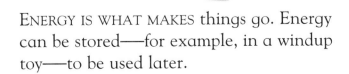

ENERGY IS WHAT MAKES things go. Energy can be stored—for example, in a windup toy—to be used later.

Can you go fast?

Try these activities to explore movement. Ask your child to try moving in different ways. Talk about which ways of moving are easy and which are difficult.

How fast can you hop on one leg? Can you hop faster on your other leg?

How fast can you run? Are you faster or slower than your friends?

Can you spin around quickly? What happens when you stand still after spinning?

Scientific Principles

Energy is what makes things move. It makes the muscles contract, which then provides the force needed to make the body move. Fast movements need more energy than slower movements.

Can you do a forward roll? Can you roll fast?

Can you roll backward? Which is harder to do?

Can you make it go?

Discover different ways of making things move. Ask your child to try bouncing a ball, flicking a coin, and playing with a yo-yo. Talk about why some ways of making things go are easier than others.

How far can you kick a ball? Can you make the ball go farther if you throw it?

For how long can you keep a balloon in the air using your head?

How many skittles can you bowl over with one ball?

Scientific Principles

Energy can be transferred from a person to an object to make it move. The muscles of the arm and foot provide the force needed to push the ball or balloon. These muscles gain the energy they need to move from the food we eat. When an object is moving, its energy can be transferred to another object. This is what happens when a moving ball hits pins and knocks them over.

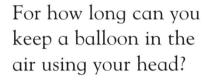

Will air make it go?

Play these games to see how air makes things move. Ask your child if he or she can control the way an object moves by blowing harder or more gently.

Can you use a paper fan to make sheets of paper move?

Can you build a Hovercraft? Ask an adult to cut a hole in a shoe-box lid. Push a tube through the hole. What happens when you blow down the tube?

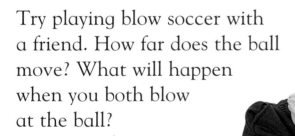

Try playing blow soccer with a friend. How far does the ball move? What will happen when you both blow at the ball?

Scientific Principles

The movement of the fan causes the air to move, which in turn makes the paper move. When you blow air down the Hovercraft tube, the force of the air pushing against the ground makes the Hovercraft move. When two people blow a ball in opposite directions, the force of the two opposing air flows can equal each other out, so the ball does not move.

Children with asthma may need to be supervised for blowing activities.

Will it fly?

Discover different ways of making things fly through the air. Talk about which objects will fly. Ask your child which things fly better than others.

Can you keep a kite in the air? How high can you make it go?

Can you make a paper airplane fly quickly? Try making paper airplanes of different sizes. Which plane travels farthest?

Can you skim a paper plate through the air? How far can you make it go?

Try making a helicopter from a rectangular piece of thin cardboard. Cut and fold it like this and fix a paper clip to the middle flap. Throw the helicopter up into the air. What happens now?

Scientific Principles

The force of gravity pulls all objects toward the Earth. An object with a large surface area, such as a kite, falls to the ground more slowly because the force of the air is pushing against its large surface.

Will water make it go?

Carry out these activities to see how water can make things go. Encourage your child to experiment with a powerful and a weak jet of water. Talk about how changing the flow of water affects how an object moves.

Can you move a plastic plate with the jet from a hose? How can you make a boat move by splashing? Can you make it go forward and backward?

Try making a waterwheel from a circle of thin cardboard and a pencil. Ask an adult to help make cuts in the circle, to fold the flaps, and to push a pencil through the center. What happens when you pour water over the waterwheel? What happens when you hold the waterwheel under a running tap?

Scientific Principles

The moving water provides the force to move the plate or waterwheel. The stronger the force, the faster the plate or wheel will move. A very weak jet of water may not have enough force to move an object.

What makes it go?

Try out these experiments to discover different ways to make things move. Ask your child to look at her toys and figure out what makes them go. Look at clockwork toys that need to be wound up and at toys with electric motors.

Can you use a magnet to make things go?

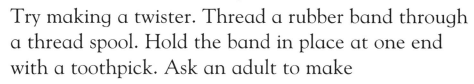

Try making a twister. Thread a rubber band through a thread spool. Hold the band in place at one end with a toothpick. Ask an adult to make a hole through the middle of a slice of candle. Thread the free end of the band through the candle slice. Then push a pencil through the band. Wind up the elastic band, using the pencil to turn it. Put the twister on the floor.

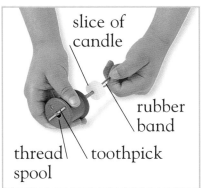

slice of candle

rubber band

thread spool

toothpick

Scientific Principles

Some metals will move when attracted by the pulling force of a magnet. The twister works by using stored energy, like a clockwork toy. When you wind up the rubber band, you store energy in the twister. When you let go, the stored energy makes the rubber band move, which then provides the force to move the twister.

What happens when you let go of the twister?

Can you make it roll?

Carry out these experiments to discover which things will roll. Let your child experiment with some objects that will roll, some, such as a cone, that will roll in an odd way, and some, such as a cube, that will not roll at all.

Collect a range of objects with different shapes. Which object rolls best along the floor?

Rest a toy track over a few cushions to make a slope. Which things roll best along the track?

How far can you go on a scooter? Is it easier to go up or down a slope?

Do you have any toys with wheels? Do the toys roll best on a flat surface or on a slope?

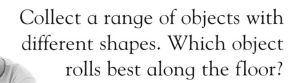

Scientific Principles

Friction is generated when two materials come into contact and oppose one another. It can slow things down. Objects that roll overcome friction more efficiently than objects that do not roll.

Does it go quickly or slowly?

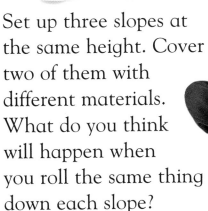

Try out these activities to introduce the idea of speed. Talk about which objects move quickly and which go slowly. Ask your child how she can change the speed at which things go.

Can you make a marble roll quickly in a tube? How can you make the marble roll very slowly?

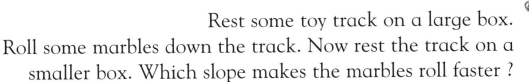

Rest some toy track on a large box. Roll some marbles down the track. Now rest the track on a smaller box. Which slope makes the marbles roll faster ?

Set up three slopes at the same height. Cover two of them with different materials. What do you think will happen when you roll the same thing down each slope?

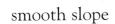

smooth slope   slope with carpet   slope with matting

Scientific Principles

The marble experiments show that changing the gradient of the slope alters the rate at which the marble rolls. The different surfaces on the three slopes create varying amounts of friction, so the same object rolls at a different speed down each slope.

Magnets and Batteries

These experiments encourage young children to find out about static electricity and magnetism, as they create static charges, use magnets, and build simple circuits.

Children can discover that:

FRICTION ON SOME OBJECTS can create an electrostatic charge, which may attract or repel other charged objects.

MAGNETS HAVE NORTH AND SOUTH POLES, which attract opposite poles and repel like poles. Magnets will only attract objects made of some metals.

A SIMPLE CIRCUIT CAN BE made with a battery and wires. The circuit will make a light bulb, buzzer, or motor work.

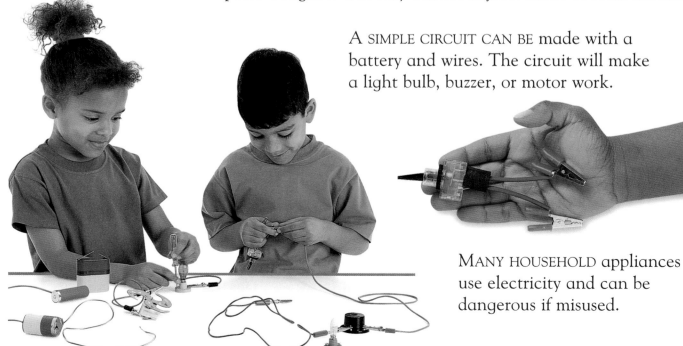

MANY HOUSEHOLD appliances use electricity and can be dangerous if misused.

What happens if you rub it?

Try these experiments to create an electrostatic charge in an object. Ask your child if he can feel the two charges pull toward each other. Do two charges sometimes push away from each other?

Rub a balloon against your clothes. What happens when you hold it close to someone's hair?

What will happen if you hold a rubbed balloon against a wall and let go?

Scientific Principles

When some materials are rubbed, an electric charge is generated. If the charge cannot flow through the material, it remains on the surface as static electricity. If two materials are rubbed, their electric charges may cause them to attract or repel each other.

What happens if you rub a plastic ruler with a plastic bag and hold the ruler over small pieces of paper? Now try rubbing the ruler with silk or cotton material.

What does a magnet do?

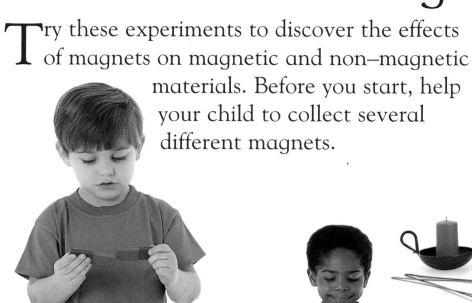

Try these experiments to discover the effects of magnets on magnetic and non–magnetic materials. Before you start, help your child to collect several different magnets.

What do you feel when you hold two magnets end to end? What happens if you turn one around?

Scientific Principles

Magnets have an effect on some materials and not on others. They only attract objects containing certain metals, such as iron or steel. A magnet has two poles called north and south. When the north and south poles of a pair of magnets are close together, they attract each other. When the poles are the same, they repel each other.

What happens when you hold your magnet near toys and other objects in the room?

What will happen when you hang two magnets side by side on strings?

Which things will not stick to a magnet?

Can you make a magnet?

Play these games to see if you can make a magnet. Ask your child if one magnet can be used to make another magnet.

Can you make a spoon into a magnet? Rub the spoon with one end of a magnet for a long time.

How will you know if the spoon is now a magnet? Bang the spoon on the ground. Is the spoon still a magnet?

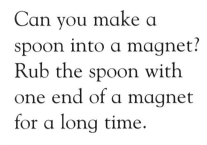

Do metal things stick to a fork? Hold a magnet on one end of the fork. Do metal things stick to the fork now? What happens if you take the magnet away?

Can you  turn a wire coat hanger into a magnet?

Scientific Principles

Permanent magnets remain magnetic all the time. Metals such as iron and steel can be made magnetic by holding a permanent magnet close to them. In this way, the fork, spoon, and wire coat hanger can all be made into magnets. If magnets are dropped or knocked, their magnetism may be lost.

How strong is a magnet?

Try these experiments to find out how strong your magnets are. Are some magnets stronger than others? Ask your child what the biggest object is that she can pick up with a magnet.

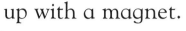

How many paper clips can you pick up with one magnet? Now try with two magnets. Can you pick up more?

Will a magnet work if you wrap it in cloth, paper, or aluminum foil? Will it work through wood?

Will your magnet work through water? Can you get paper clips out of a plastic bottle of water without getting your fingers wet?

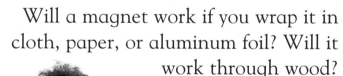

Scientific Principles

Different magnets are of different strengths and will attract metal objects from various distances. Some magnets have a force strong enough to affect heavy objects and to work through thick materials.

Fix a magnet to the floor with sticky tape. How close to the magnet can you push small metal objects before they are pulled toward it?

Can you use a magnet?

Play these games to find out what magnets can be used for. Discover how a magnet can make a compass. Talk about what we use compasses for.

Cut out lots of paper fish and fix a paper clip onto each one. Make a fishing rod with some string, a magnet, and a stick. How many fish can you catch in one try?

Hang a magnet on a piece of string. Then use a compass to find out which way the magnet points. Do all magnets point the same way?

Make a sewing needle into a magnet by rubbing it with a magnet. Now float a small plastic lid in a bowl of water and put the needle on it. Can you say which way is north?

Scientific Principles

When a magnet is suspended, one end of the magnet will always point to magnetic north. This is because the Earth itself is a huge magnet and attracts another magnet's north-seeking pole.

Be careful when using a needle.

What does a battery do?

Try these experiments to find out about common batteries. Show your child how to insert batteries into a device. Ask how we would know when something needs new batteries.

Look closely at the batteries you have. In what ways are they all the same?

Do you have any batteries like the ones shown here? How many different shapes and sizes can you find?

Scientific Principles

Batteries generate electric current and provide a force to push the current around a circuit. In order to make things work, the batteries must be inserted in a particular way. Common batteries are safe to use for these experiments. Do not use 9-volt, nickel cadmium, or rechargeable batteries.

control panel for battery operated car

flashlight

contact inside flashlight

cassette player

battery operated dog

calculator

watch

personal stereo

Can you make things work by putting batteries into them? Can you use any battery to make a flashlight work? How many batteries do different things need? Where do you put the batteries? What will happen if you put the batteries in the other way around?

Never try to cut open a battery.

Can you make a circuit?

Find out what things are needed to make a small bulb light up. Discover which materials conduct an electric current and which do not.

Can you join together some wires, a battery, and a light bulb in a holder? Where do the ends of the wires go?

alligator clip

wire

bulb holder

Will the light bulb light up?

Will the light bulb work if you add a plastic ruler into the circuit? What happens if you use a metal fork instead of the ruler?

battery

Can you use string instead of wires to make a circuit?

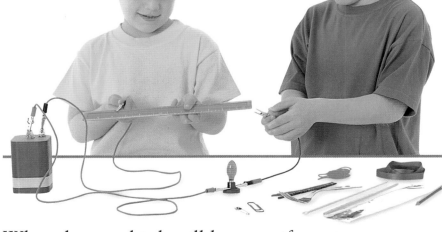

Scientific Principles

A circuit is a complete path of material, such as metal wire, that conducts an electric current when connected to a battery. This electric current can make small devices work.

What do you think will happen if you try some of the things on the table in your circuit?

Can you make a big circuit?

Discover how to make switches and buzzers work, and how to operate two or more devices at the same time. Follow the path that an electric current takes around a big circuit.

switch

buzzer

How can you make two light bulbs light up at the same time? Can you add a switch to turn them on and off?

Can you make a buzzer work?

Draw a fan shape onto some cardboard and cut it out. Push the fan onto the motor spindle. Can you make the motor turn the fan?

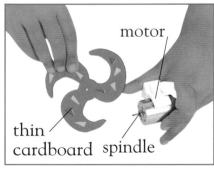

motor

thin cardboard spindle

○ Scientific
■ Principles

A complete circuit is needed before a device such as a bulb, buzzer, or motor will work. A switch controls the flow of electric current.

Can you build a big circuit to make a fan spin around at the same time as a bulb lights up?

Building Things

These experiments encourage young children to investigate the properties of wood, metal, plastic, and a range of familiar materials. Children are asked to look for similarities and differences in materials, and to study their textures, strengths, flexibility, and uses.

Children can discover that:

MATTER EXISTS IN three states – solid, liquid, and gas.

ALL MATERIALS HAVE different properties, some of which, such as strength, flexibility, or hardness, enable them to be used for specific purposes, such as building.

SOME MATERIALS occur naturally, while others have to be manufactured from raw materials.

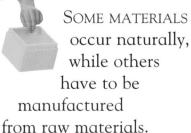

SOME MATERIALS CAN BE recycled, e.g., aluminum drink cans, which can be collected after use and the aluminum processed to be used again.

What is it made of?

Try these activities to explore what things are made of. Ask your child to collects lots of everyday objects. Explain that things are made out of different materials. Can he tell what the objects are made of by looking at them and feeling them?

What sorts of things are made of wood? What objects are made from metal? Close your eyes and try to pick out all the metal objects. What are the other things made of?

How many different objects can you find that are made of plastic? Are all plastics the same?

Can you find some solid things? Can you find some gases? Can you find some liquids?

Scientific Principles

Objects are made out of different materials, which can be solids, liquids, or gases. Materials can be identified by the way they look and by the properties they possess.

What is it like?

Study a range of objects with your child and try to describe them. Encourage your child to use her senses to examine the objects' physical properties. Discuss which words can be used for describing the objects.

Which objects feel rough?
Which things feel smooth?
What is the smoothest thing you can find?

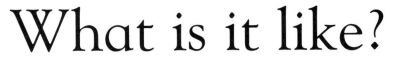

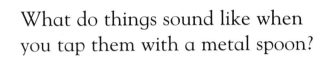

What do things sound like when you tap them with a metal spoon?

Can you find some heavy things? What things are light? What is the heaviest thing you can find?

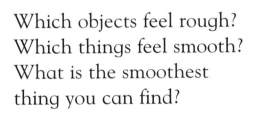

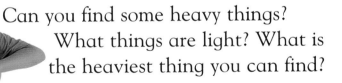

What sorts of things feel cold?
Do some things feel warm?

Scientific Principles

Different materials have different physical properties, which we can discover using our senses.

109

What can you do to it?

Try these experiments on a variety of materials to see what happens to them. Talk about different actions, such as bouncing, squashing, and bending. Discuss the effects these actions can have on the objects.

Can you find any of these things? Which ones bounce the best? Try bouncing them on different surfaces, such as on a carpet or a hard floor.

beach ball

beanbag

juggling ball

sponge

plastic ball

soft rubber ball

tennis ball

eraser

marble

pom-pom

wax

wood

Which is the hardest thing to scratch with a nail? Which is the easiest?

plastic

stone

chalk

metal

Scientific Principles

Applying force to materials in a variety of ways affects the materials differently according to their physical properties. Some materials can be compressed easily, some are very flexible, and others extremely hard.

Find a plastic ruler, a metal ruler, and a wooden ruler. Which one bends the most?

Is it strong or weak?

Discover how we can tell which things are strong and which are weak. What can happen to weak things? Talk about the strong materials used for buildings, such as bricks, wood, and glass.

Find some cloth, plastic, aluminum foil, and different sorts of paper. Which of these is the hardest to fold?

Which sort of material tears most easily? How many times can you fold a sheet of paper in half?

How many bricks does it take to squash the sides of a tube? Can you squash a tube if you stand it on end?

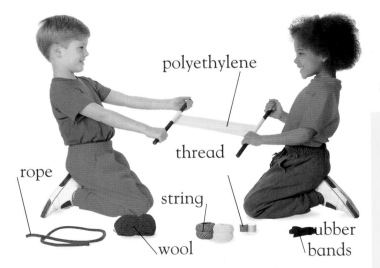

polyethylene

thread

rope

string

wool

rubber bands

Ask a friend to help you test these things. What will happen if you fix each thing between two sticks and pull?

Scientific Principles

The strength of materials is revealed when force is applied to them. When you stand a tube on end, the tube is stronger and is therefore harder to squash. Whatever the size, thickness, or strength of the paper used, it cannot be folded in half more than eight times.

Is it made in a factory?

Ask your child to collect a variety of objects that we might use or eat. Look at her collection and talk about what sorts of things are made in a factory, and what sorts of things occur naturally. Talk about whether an object would be thrown away or recycled once it is finished with.

What things can you find that are made in a factory?

How many things can you find that come from nature?

Look at a collection of food and drink and their containers. Can you say which foods and drinks go in which containers? What are the food containers made of? Which containers are thrown away after use? Which ones are used again?

cereal

water

juice burger soft drink coffee tomatoes

Scientific Principles

There are materials that occur naturally, and there are substances, such as plastics, that are manufactured from raw materials. Certain materials are used for specific tasks because of the properties they possess.

Can you build things?

Try out these activities to discover a variety of ways to build towers and walls. Talk about which methods of building create the strongest, most stable structures. Experiment with small adjustments to increase the strength of the buildings.

Can you build a tower with drinking straws? How many straws will you use? How can you make your tower stronger?

Can you build a tall tower with some flowerpots? How high does your tower get before it falls over?

Scientific Principles

Widening the base of the straw tower will give it a lower center of gravity and make it more stable. The brick wall is stronger if the bricks are positioned to overlap the joints.

Which way of building with blocks makes the strongest wall? Roll a ball against your walls to test them.

Can you make materials?

Try to make some building materials by mixing and shaping different ingredients. Ask your child to vary the proportions of the ingredients, and see how this affects the final materials. Try testing the materials by rubbing them with sandpaper. Which is the hardest material?

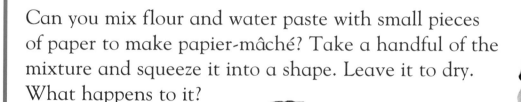

Can you mix flour and water paste with small pieces of paper to make papier-mâché? Take a handful of the mixture and squeeze it into a shape. Leave it to dry. What happens to it?

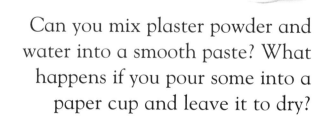

Can you shape a lump of clay into a brick? Now leave it to dry. Which brick dries more quickly, a small one or a large one?

Can you mix plaster powder and water into a smooth paste? What happens if you pour some into a paper cup and leave it to dry?

Scientific Principles

Materials can be made by combining different ingredients. Varying the proportions of the ingredients can alter the qualities of the material.

Always wear a dust mask when you use sandpaper or handle fine powders.

Can you change things?

Try these activities to find out if you can make things change. Discuss with your child which changes are permanent and which can be reversed. Ask your child to think about how different materials will change when soaked in water.

Do materials change if you make them wet? Which material will be best for making an umbrella?

Can you change the color of things with paint? Which materials are hard to paint? Will adding glue to the paint make a difference?

nails

lentils

aluminum foil   wool   wood   plastic

What will happen if you leave different materials to soak in water for a few days?

Scientific Principles

Some materials will absorb water, while others are water resistant or waterproof. Some materials are changed when soaked in water or sanded, and some of these changes are reversible. Building materials are materials such as wood, nails, plastics, and bricks that cannot easily be changed by water.

Glossary

Air
A mixture of gases and vapors that surrounds the Earth.

Air pressure
The force that is exerted by air as it pushes down on objects.

Astronomy
The study of stars and planets.

Atmosphere
The layer of air that surrounds a planet.

Balancing point
The point at which an object will balance and not topple.

Birds
A group of animals that are covered with feathers and lay eggs.

Camouflage
The way that an animal's coloring merges with the background.

Capacity
The amount (volume) that a vessel can hold.

Center of gravity
The point at which all the mass of an object seems to be concentrated. It is also called the center of mass.

Chromatography
The process by which an absorbent material separates a mixture of chemicals in solution.

Circuit
The path around which an electric current can flow.

Cloud
A mass of water vapor or ice crystals that stays at more or less the same altitude.

Condensation
The process by which a vapor or gas cools and changes into a liquid.

Decay
A process by which microbes such as fungi and bacteria feed on dead materials.

Energy
The ability to make things happen or go.

Environment
Different places in which living things can survive, e.g., the ocean, the land.

Erosion
The process by which one material is broken down by the continuous rubbing of another material, e.g., particles in water can erode rock.

Evaporation
The process by which liquids are heated and changed into a vapor or gas.

Fish
A group of animals that are covered by flexible scales, live in water, and breathe using gills.

Force
The pushes or pulls that make objects start to move, speed up, change directions, slow down, and stop. The twists and squeezes that change the shape of an object.

Freezing
The process of removing heat from a substance so that it changes from a liquid into a solid, e.g., water into ice.

Friction
The force that slows down or stops the movement of one surface against another.

Gas
Material that has no fixed shape or volume.

Gradient
A slope.

Gravity
A force that pulls objects toward each other, e.g., toward the Earth or Moon.

Habitat
The part of the environment where animals or plants live, e.g., freshwater pond, rain forest.

Inanimate
Never has been alive.

Insulator
A material that reduces or blocks the flow of heat, electricity, or sound.

Life cycle
All the stages in the life of an animal or plant.

Lift
The upward force of an airplane's wing that keeps it in the air.

Light
A form of energy that is given off by a light source, e.g., the Sun, a flame, a bulb. It can be detected by the eye.

Liquid
Material that can flow to fill a space and can be poured.

Magnetic north
The direction in which the north-seeking pole of a suspended magnet always points.

Magnetism
The invisible force of attraction or repulsion between some materials, particularly iron.

Mammals
A group of animals that have hair and feed their young on milk.

Mass
The amount of matter in an object. It is measured in kilograms or pounds.

Matter
Anything that has mass and occupies a space.

Melting
The process of heating matter so that it changes from a solid into a liquid.

Opaque
A material that will not let light pass through it.

Organ
A part of the body of an animal or plant that performs a particular job.

Pitch
The sensation of how high or how deep a sound is.

Prism
A block of transparent material with a triangular cross section. Prisms can split light to produce a spectrum.

Reptiles
A group of air-breathing animals that have scales on their body and lay eggs.

Resistance
The measure of how much a material opposes the flow of an electrical current.

Senses
The means by which animals detect changes around them.

Shadow
A dark region formed when an opaque object is placed in front of a light source.

Sight
The sense that detects changes in light.

Skeleton
A framework that supports an animal, provides anchor points for muscles to help it move, and protects the inner organs.

Smell
The sense that detects chemicals in the air.

Solid
Material that retains its shape, and cannot be compressed.

Solution
A mixture of a solid or gas dissolved in a liquid.

Sound
The vibrations of a solid, liquid, or gas that are detected and heard by the ear.

Static charge
When some materials are rubbed together, they produce an electric charge on the surface.

Taste
The sense that detects chemicals in a solution.

Thermometer
An instrument used to measure temperature.

Timbre
The quality of sounds produced by different materials.

Touch
The sense that detects pressure.

Translucent
A material that allows some light through but cannot be seen through.

Transparent
A material that allows light through and can be seen through.

Vapor
A type of gas that can be turned into a liquid by changing the pressure.

Weight
The force with which a mass is pulled toward the center of the Earth. The unit of weight is the newton.

Index

Equipment

Here is a general list of useful equipment you could collect from around the house before getting started on the experiments.

Aluminum foil

Balls
Balloons
Batteries
Books
Broom
Buckets
Building blocks

Cardboard
Cardboard tubes
Coins
Corks
Cushions

Drinking straws

Forks

Magnets
Marbles
Modeling clay

Newspaper

Paints

Paper
Paper clips
Paper cups
Paper plates
Pencil
Plain flour
Plastic bottles
Plastic flowerpots
Plastic lids

Rubber bands
Ruler

Sandpaper
Scissors
Shoe box
Spoons
Sticky tape
String

Thread spools
Toothpicks
Toy cars
Trays

Wool

Magnets and Batteries

You can get the following simple equipment in a hardware or general electrical store:

Thin wires
Small light bulb in a holder
Small switch
Buzzer
Small motor
Alligator clips